***Or wife, or spouse, or partner, or significant other, or...**

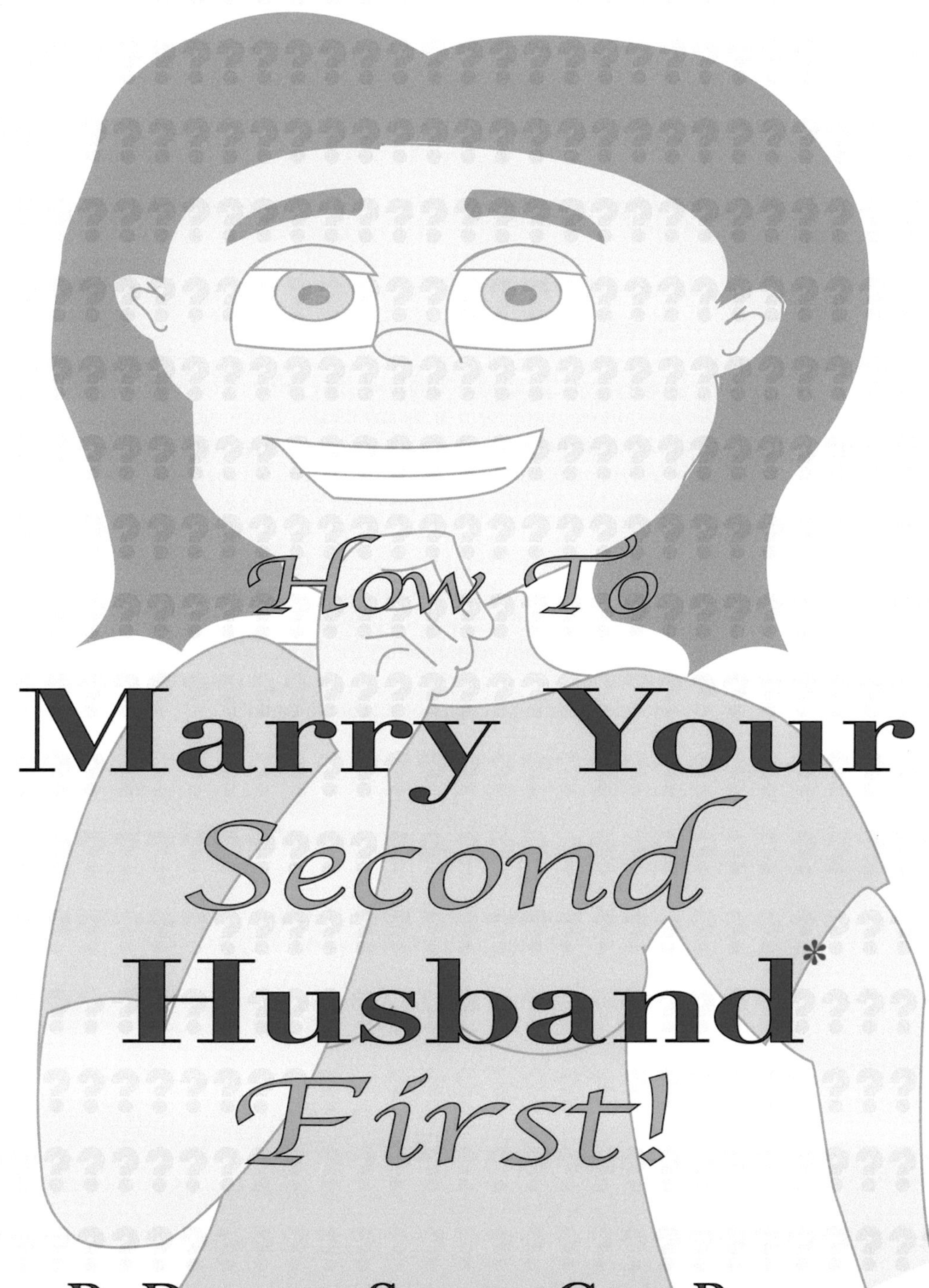

How To Marry Your Second Husband* First!

By Didi and Steven Carr Reuben

Illustrations by Seth Mallios

To order additional copies of this book, contact:

Xlibris
844-714-8691
www.Xlibris.com
Orders@Xlibris.com

ISBN:	Softcover	978-1-6641-3220-7
	EBook	978-1-6641-3219-1

Print information available on the last page

Rev. date: 11/23/2020

CONTENTS

This book is dedicated to all those looking for "The One" with whom to share their life.

PREFACE

If we had a dollar for every time someone said to us, "If I only knew then what I know now, I never would have married my first husband," we'd probably be the richest clergy couple in America! For over forty years as a rabbi, Steven has counseled thousands of couples of all ages and backgrounds who have come to him for relationship advice. For the past 36 years of our marriage together, as Steven's life partner, Didi has been serving as informal counselor, guide, and assertive training teacher to adults and youth alike, and for years wrote a popular "Dear Abby" type column ("Dear Rebbetzin Didi") dispensing personal advice and support to couples and individuals of all ages.

Friends, acquaintances, fellow clergy and their spouses, and members of our extended congregational family who have seen how well our relationship works have been "noodging" us for years to put down in writing our unique recipe for a successful marriage. Up until recently Steven has been working full time as Senior Rabbi of a 1,000 family congregation in Los Angeles, but now that he has retired and become "Rabbi Emeritus," he has time to do the things he couldn't do before – exercise, play drums, create a non-profit to address intimate partner abuse in the Jewish community, and write this book! Our particular brand of down-to-earth relationship advice is a blend of humor and experience, both personal and professional, and is based upon the stories and life lessons of our own and those of hundreds of other couples who have been willing to share their experiences and insights with us over the years. Enjoy!

Didi and Steven

INTRODUCTION

If you had a friend who announced one day that she intended to go to Las Vegas, stroll up to the first roulette table she could find and then bet her entire personal fortune on either "red" or "black," you would know for sure that she had lost her mind and do whatever you could to talk her out of it. Yet nearly everyone has heard the devastating statistic that over half of all marriages in America end in divorce. So, in effect just like your crazy gambler friend every single person who steps up to the altar and says, "I do" has about as much certainty in his or her marriage decision as your misguided friend does at the roulette table.

Yet, since 2.3 million couples step up to the marriage roulette altar every year in America alone (which breaks down to at least 6,200 weddings every day), it makes you wonder just what they are thinking when they do, and what it is that makes them think that they will be the lucky ones that beat the odds? Of course, every one of them is filled with hope for the future and certain that against all odds their relationship will be one of the lucky ones that make it.

Luck doesn't have much to do with it if you possess any of the following traits that are destined to derail your relationship journey even before it begins. For example, how many of the following traits do you recognize in yourself:

1. Opinionated
2. Judgmental
3. Impatient
4. Closed-minded
5. Inflexible
6. Abusive
7. Insecure
8. Bully
9. Vengeful
10. Master manipulator

If you see yourself in any of these traits and are not willing to let go or change them in order to create a successful relationship, you might as well stop reading this book right now. If you are at least willing to change #5 - "Inflexible" then there is still a chance that by reading this book and taking our suggestions to heart you will be motivated to change your negative traits into the positive traits that will attract the kind of partner you desire. Seeing yourself in any of the traits on this list is already a sign that half the battle is already won. The next step in winning the war to create lasting love in your life is figuring out how to change them into the positive traits that will serve you instead. After all, the willingness to recognize bad habits and dysfunctional traits in the first place and not simply stay stuck in the "blame game" of always thinking that the failure of any previous relationships was all "his" fault, or "her" fault is a tremendous sign of maturity and your willingness to take responsibility for the life that you intend to create going forward.

What has inspired the writing of this book is our knowledge that most people don't realize how easy it really is to have a successful relationship. With all the hundreds of books, DVD's, weekend retreats, private therapy, and television talk shows dedicated to exposing the trials, tribulations, and traumas of dating, marriage, breaking up and divorce, is it any wonder that the average man or woman of any age today is convinced that creating and sustaining a successful relationship or marriage must be one of the hardest challenges in the world? We have written this simple, hopefully entertaining, easy-to-understand guide to demonstrate to anyone and everyone, that CREATING A SUCCESSFUL MARRIAGE IS AS EASY AS ONE, TWO, THREE.

ONE – forget everything that everyone has told you over and over again about how difficult it is to find and keep a successful relationship. TWO – use our simple guide to identify the RED LIGHTS that will warn you what to avoid and the RED LIGHTS that tell you what you or your partner need to STOP doing to yourselves and one another. THREE – follow our simple guide to understanding the GREEN LIGHTS that signal "YES," "FULL SPEED AHEAD" to a satisfying, fulfilling and successful relationship and marriage. It's that simple. Really.

The goal of this little book is to teach our truth, that there are clearly identifiable traits and characteristics of successful relationships that you can use as a yardstick against which to measure the potential success or failure of your own relationship. This book will help you to recognize those positive traits and characteristics in yourself and others and learn to apply them to create the marriage of your dreams.

Over the years of our work with couples and individuals from all walks of life, as we studied the secrets of successful marriages and loving life partnerships we have realized that even though most people have heard about the 50%+ divorce rate in America, very few realize that the odds of success with second marriages is even worse (about 60% divorce rate) than it is with first marriages. The more we thought about the implications of that statistic the more we looked to uncover the secrets to creating, nurturing and keeping a successful marriage whether it is your first, second, or third marriage. If you are already on your fourth marriage we wish we had come out with this book sooner! The results of our many years of hands-on counseling, study and interaction with hundreds of couples is exactly what you will learn in the pages of this book. You will discover the tried and true strategies for meeting the right person, asking the right questions, developing the right relationship, and creating a marriage that will last.

How to Marry Your Second Husband First is an easy guide to creating a successful marriage that draws upon not only our many years of working with others, but our own personal lives as well. Both of us have been married before. Both of us have made and learned from mistakes in the past. Together we have devised this step-by-step strategy to help you take those dreaded road blocks and pitfalls that most people tend to trip over or fall into the first time around, and turn them into the positives that help create success instead. Of course, if you are someone who has already been unsuccessfully married or lost at the committed relationship life game, this book is also for you, and will provide the tools you need to make better choices the next time around.

Getting married provides a unique opportunity to do something that is truly remarkable – you actually get to choose your "nearest" relative in life. It is such a significant decision, that the act of getting married is possibly the single most important and powerful choice you will ever make in life.

All of civilization is founded on the social unit we call "family." When most people hear the word "family," they think of biology, genetics and the idea of procreation. But the reality is that most families begin not as a result of genetics, but rather because of choice. You choose your mate. You choose to marry someone, and through that marriage you create a new family. In reality it isn't just procreation and children that make a family but rather the choice to create the marriage relationship itself that forms the foundation of all families. From a sociological perspective, what you are doing when you get married is that you are leaving the sphere of your parent's home as your primary family and creating your own primary family with your mate. If you have children, the family grows, but the children don't make the "family," the family itself begins with your marriage.

What that means is that since all of society is grounded in the institution of family, and since every family is created by the exercising of human choice in what we call marriage, then all of society itself is based on the power of one human being choosing another in marriage. That is another reason why marriage is such a powerful emotional event – subconsciously we have internalized the reality through millions of years of human and social evolution that every marriage is another crucial building block of society itself.

That is also why we have written this book. Because we believe in marriage, family, and the gift of committed life relationships. We believe that if given the right tools, most people can easily learn how to make the right decision the first time, and in effect learn how to "marry their second husband (or wife) first." It is our goal to provide insight, inspiration, and encouragement to couples of all religions, races, sexual orientations, and economic levels, so that instead of marriage being one of the greatest "crap shoots" in life, it can be what it is meant to be – the greatest source of joy, satisfaction, and love in the world.

In the most successful marriages, each partner is more authentically him or herself as a result of their relationship. In a true spiritual partnership, each person is inspired and encouraged to strive each day to become the person they see reflected in their partner's eyes. In nearly every successful marriage we know, couples will tell us the same thing – "I feel that I am a better 'me' because of our relationship."

Our goal in writing this book is to help you understand how to pick the right partner so that you will be able to create exactly that kind of empowering, inspiring, mutually fulfilling relationship. We are certain that marriage need not be a guessing game. Of course, it takes patience and understanding, humor and compassion, enthusiasm and passion. But it also takes the willingness to learn and grow, and to be open to discovering more and more about yourself as well as your partner with the passing of every day.

We believe that everyone wants intimacy, closeness, that feeling of being one with someone you love. One thing we know with absolute certainty is that there is only one road to intimacy. The only road to intimacy is over the rocky, sometimes scary road called, "vulnerability." Unfortunately, there are too many people for whom revealing their inner fears, hopes, and dreams to another is the single most terrifying idea they can imagine. Yet in our professional and personal experiences we have come to realize that the only way any one can ever experience a true sense of intimacy with another is if he or she is willing to let down his or her guard and be vulnerable. Period.

When Steven was growing up he used to watch a fabulous children's television show in Los Angeles called, "The Engineer Bill Show." Even today, nearly 70 years later, he still remembers the most important lesson that was taught by Engineer Bill every single day on his show: "On a green light you go and on a red light you stop, because no good engineer would ever run a red light!" So that's how we have organized this book as well – with RED LIGHTS and GREEN LIGHTS. On the RED LIGHTS you stop – whether it means changing your own habits, learning to do something differently than you are used to doing, or realizing that the red light is a red flag telling you that another person is not for you, as you might have originally thought. The RED LIGHTS section will give you the tools to know what and whom to avoid. On the GREEN LIGHTS you go – the book is chock filled with every behavior, attitude, and key to creating a successful relationship and marriage that you will need to insure that you will, indeed discover the secret to how to marry your second husband (or wife) first. So let's get going!

Chapter One

10 STEPS TO FINDING YOUR "SECOND HUSBAND" FIRST

"Our lives are fashioned by our choices. First we make our choices. Then our choices make us."
— Anne Frank

Ok let's begin by getting right to the point. Before we share with you the fabulous "do's" and "don'ts" of our Red Light/Green Light lists, we decided to give you the essence of the whole book right here, in ten easy lessons. Hopefully you bought the whole book in which case we thank you for helping us with our mortgage, but if you just picked this up in a friend's house and are browsing through to find out what wisdom we have to share and stumbled on this chapter, you can simply read this chapter and toss the rest and you'll be just fine. So here they are, <u>the top ten steps to finding your second husband (or wife) first:</u>

1. *Make a list of the top ten (ok, at least the top five) most important qualities you would love to have in a mate.* Here are some possible examples: charitable, kind, compassionate, generous, rich, handsome, well groomed, smells good, romantic, thoughtful, wants to live in a small town, wants to live in a big city, would make a good potential father to your future potential children, would make a good father to your present children, patient, flexible, honest, funny, playful, intelligent, scholarly, a lover of books, a musician, loves music, loves to travel, loves animals, a good lover, adventurous, loves the outdoors, has hair, doesn't have hair, is a wise investor, loves his parents (but not too much), is deeply religious, is deeply secular, a regularly church goer, sings in the

choir, wouldn't walk into a church on a bet, has been to therapy, believes in past lives, is the same religion or race as you, is in a 12 step program, likes to use recreational drugs, never uses recreational drugs, wants children, doesn't want children, has good health insurance, is an artist, has lots of close childhood friends.

2. *Look over your list and see how many of the qualities that you seek in a "Second Husband" you also possess yourself.*
3. *Make a decision to become the kind of person you are seeking so that you will naturally attract that exact kind of person.* You can hardly expect to attract someone with the qualities on your list without possessing those qualities yourself. Well, actually you can certainly ignore this advice (or any of the other advice we are sharing), but your chances of finding someone with the qualities you desire will definitely improve the more you exhibit those qualities yourself. Simply put, like tends to attract like.
4. *Make a list of the traits you couldn't possibly live with in a "Second Husband."* You know, the "deal breakers" like too little hair, too much hair, one brow, cheapskate, always late to pick you up, always late to leave for important events, someone who puts you down, someone who disparages your achievements, someone who is jealous of your other relationships and friends, inconsiderate, disrespectful of you, or of women in general, treated his ex-wife badly in a divorce, hates his mother, has bad breath, spits when he talks, puts his mother on a pedestal, eats with his mouth open, always interrupts you when you are talking, smokes, eats with his hands (and you are not in a Moroccan restaurant), is a Republican, is a Democrat, is totally disinterested in politics, is uncharitable, a stingy tipper, a disgustingly over-tipper, speaks rudely to those who serve him, has small feet (well, you know), terrible in bed, always talks about himself, has relatives with whom he never speaks, hates animals, has animals, hates to travel, is always on the road for his work, likes shag carpeting.
5. *Stick to your guns.* Do not compromise the most important character traits of Lists #1 and #4. Each trait compromised is a giant step closer to marrying the dreaded "First Husband" instead of marrying your "Second Husband" first.
6. *Get involved as a volunteer in a non-profit, charitable organization that deals with an issue that is close to your heart*, like helping with the homeless (www.lafh.org & www.theadvotproject.org), education of inner-city kids, cancer/AIDS groups, literacy programs, raising funds to end world hunger or specific diseases. This will help take your mind off the feeling of desperation to find a mate while at the same time giving you a whole new feeling of meaning and purpose to your life. Plus, the real bonus is that it will expose you to other people who are giving and loving like yourself and who share a passion for making a difference in the world. What a perfect way to meet a "Second Spouse" first.

7. *Become happy with yourself just the way you are.* Be happy with the way you look, feel and act in the world. Remember, you have a choice here. Just get out there and DO whatever you need to do to get happy in all these ways. You may need to start exercising, eating better, taking classes to improve your mind, whatever. When you are happy with yourself, it shows. People want to be around a happy person, it is literally contagious and attractive. People don't want to be around a sad, negative, or judgy person, and you don't want to be around a person like that either. Good lesson to remember.
8. *Don't panic.* Avoid the "Biological Clock Syndrome" like the plague. In our experience, it appears that women with feelings of desperation due to the old biological clock ticking away relentlessly in their ear, tend to marry settling for just "good enough" rather than waiting as long as it takes to find their actual soul mate. Hey, it's the twenty-first century. These days you no longer need a first husband to have a child, you can always just hop on over to the sperm "bank" of your choice and withdraw one!
9. *Put yourself out there.* For example, everyone has a spiritual side. Find something that encourages and nourishes your sense of spirituality. Try joining a religious or spiritual group that speaks to you because that is exactly where you are likely to find your like-minded soul mate. Don't forget your soul mate is out there right now looking for you asking the same questions and checking out the same places. The trick is (and this is where luck comes in) to be there at the same time as your soul mate. Shop around. You never know what or whom you will discover as you are "shopping." Religious and spiritual gatherings of all kinds exist in your home town and just might be the perfect place to find both meaning and a sense of belonging while on your search for "The One." Also, yoga classes, Pilates and martial arts classes are not only good for your health but help to clear your cluttered mind and bring a greater sense of clarity and well-being in every sense of the word, as well.

10. *Finally, remember that finding a life mate isn't about what anybody wants but you!* This is your life and your journey and it is up to you and you alone to determine what you are looking for, what will bring you joy, happiness and fulfillment in life, what qualities are the "must haves" and what traits are the "must not haves" in your relationships and your life.

Chapter Two

RED LIGHT/GREEN LIGHT

"Because no good engineer would ever run a red light"
— Engineer Bill

Well here we are at the real fun part of this book. Our famous "Red Light/Green Light" lists. We know we said at the beginning of Chapter One that you could just read that chapter and you'd get all you really need to know about how to go about finding your second husband first, but really, if you just read this chapter you will have all the tools you will ever need to find the right mate or partner too. Look how easy we made this book! Just read chapter one and you got it, or now just read chapter two and you got it. What could be easier than that? Since we love lists (and after all who would want to be listless?), before we give you the red light and green light lists, we have yet another list – The "20 Worst Reasons for Getting Married" list. Too often over the years we have seen good hearted, otherwise intelligent and thoughtful people leap into bad marriages for all the wrong reasons. Not that leaping into bad marriages for all the right reasons works either. There are so many social pressures to get married, so many times when people just feel lonely or scared or anxious about the passing of time or suffering from the now infamous "FOMO" disease ("fear of missing out"), that they grab the first person that is even fairly decent or less offensive than the rest or simply the first person who showed an interest at all, and jump into marriage. To help you stave off that marriage craving that leads to irrational decisions and bad judgment, here is our list of the "20 Worst Reasons for Getting Married":

1. I'm broke
2. I'm tired of working
3. All my friends are getting married
4. It's time to have a baby
5. I need a father for my child
6. I'm lonely
7. I need someone to protect me
8. I want to move out of my parent's house
9. "He asked"
10. It's better for my taxes

11. I hate dating
12. I'm afraid of becoming an "old maid" (or the male version)
13. I already bought the dress
14. I'm too embarrassed to back out now
15. I can have sex whenever I want it
16. Everyone will think I'm a loser if I don't get married
17. I don't know how to end my relationship
18. Because my mother told me to do it
19. Because my mother told me not to do it
20. Isn't that what I'm supposed to do next? (First comes love, then comes…)

Extra credit: write in three more reasons of your own NOT to get married…

21.
22.
23.

Great list right? So now that you know the twenty worst reasons that people jump into marriage, here is a more comprehensive tool for assessing the chances of your next (or first) marriage being successful. If you simply use our Red Light list to look for the telltale warning signs that you should avoid at all costs and our Green Light list as a helpful look for affirming that this one is <u>the</u> one for you, things are much more likely to turn out exactly the way you dream they will. Remember it is just like Steven learned as a child from watching Engineer Bill on his children's television show: "On a red light you stop and on a green light you go, because no good engineer would ever run a red light."

Red Lights

1. He talks about himself more than he asks about you
2. You have a culture clash – "I hate/love opera, jazz, museums, sports…"
3. He has a Masters degree in procrastination – "promises, promises, promises"
4. He is a "blacksmith," always telling you "I have a lot of irons in the fire"
5. His parents had a terrible marriage and they are his life role models
6. He keeps talking about his first wife or last relationship
7. He brings his mom along on the date
8. He still lives with his parents
9. He has friends you don't want to be friends with
10. He is a trust fund baby – doesn't work or have direction or life goals
11. He buys snacks at the movie theatre and doesn't offer you any
12. He is insulting to waiters and people who serve him

13. He is a stingy tipper or he grossly over tips
14. He always wants to split the check
15. He "forgets" his wallet
16. His phone keeps ringing during dinner and he answers it
17. His on-line profile looks nothing like he looks in person
18. He lied on his profile (thinner, younger, more accomplished, more degrees)
19. He treated his Ex poorly in the divorce
20. He claims he doesn't smoke but the ashtray in his car is dirty and his breath smells like he just sprayed it with Lysol
21. He lies about his age
22. He tells you he's never been married but you keep running into small children who call him "daddy"

23. He won't talk about his ex-wife or marriage when you ask
24. He smokes, he spits, he farts
25. Think twice before marrying someone who begins a sentence with, "One of my ex wives..." or "As my mother always says..."

26. If he leaves her for you, there's a good chance he will leave you for someone else
27. What you don't want to hear after saying "I Do" – "I invited my mother to move in with us," or "Did I forget to mention I don't want children?"
28. Ask yourself, "Would I want this man (or woman) to parent a child with me?
29. You hear yourself saying, "Well, there just aren't any really great guys out there any more" or "All the great guys are already taken," clearly "settling"
30. When you ask yourself if it would be ok with you if he wasn't in your life, you answer "yes, but…"
31. You are embarrassed to introduce him to your parents or best friend
32. You keep thinking of reasons not to see him till tomorrow
33. He is uncomfortable around kids and animals
34. He doesn't keep his agreements or commitments to others (why would he keep them to you?)
35. He picks you up late habitually
36. He tells jokes that put down women or ethnic minorities
37. He gets frustrated when you don't know what he wants, even though he doesn't tell you ("mind reading syndrome")
38. He keeps saying, "Remember when we went to Mount Rushmore (or Hawaii, or saw a movie)" but that was with another woman or ex-wife.
39. He "forgot" to tell you that he has kids from a former relationship – turns out his "nephew" is really his son
40. You keep telling yourself, "Once we are married he will change" and other fairy tales

Extra Credit: Add three more "Red Lights" of your own…

41.
42.
43.

Well that was our "Red Light" list and we hope it helps put things in perspective for you. We'll apologize in advance for the fact that the Red Light list is much longer than the Green Light list and that we probably could have just said, "Look for the opposite" and been done with it. We guess it's because there are lots of things to watch out for and be warned against and if your person has even half of the qualities on the Green Light list you got yourself a winner. But seriously folks, while we are on the "Red Light" subject, it's never, ever ok for someone you are dating to 1) touch you inappropriately or without your consent, 2) talk down to you with disrespect or with verbal insults, 3) make you feel in any way stupid, 4) encourage you to become isolated from family or friends, 5) pressure you to tell him where you are and who you are with at all times, 6) force you to have sex or do something you don't want to do physically, 7) insist on taking control of your money or finances. All of the above are classic symptoms of domestic abuse and should cause you to run away as far and as fast as you can. We don't want to scare you to death, but domestic violence is the number one cause of injury to women in America (as in every 9 seconds a woman is assaulted or beaten) so please take care of yourself and if necessary call the National Dating Abuse Helpline (866) 331-9474 or National Domestic Violence Hotline (800) 799-7233. OK, so now on to the good stuff.

GREEN LIGHTS

1. You share cultural interests – art, museums, jazz, opera, football, soccer, sports, rock

2. He likes going out at night/staying in at night like you (similar biorhythm)
3. He is humble
4. You've learned to "fail your way to success" – (learned from past mistakes)
5. He treats you with excitement as if you are "the other woman"

6. He is courteous to strangers
7. He is thoughtful of others
8. He treats waiters, busboys, servers with respect
9. You like to be with his friends
10. He grew up with sisters
11. He is generous to you and also philanthropic
12. He opens the car door for you
13. He pulls out your chair
14. He insists on paying for dinner
15. He turns off his phone during dinner
16. You made a list "What kind of person am I worthy of?" and it matched your date
17. He surprises you with flowers, candy, a smoothie or a puppy (rescue)

18. You are excited about the idea of having him be the father of your child
19. You would be proud to introduce him to your parents, friends or colleagues
20. He has become your best friend
21. You love the relationship his parents have with each other
22. You admire and respect him
23. He is comfortable around kids and they like him too
24. He keeps his agreements and commitments to others whether at work or with friends and certainly with you
25. He treats other women with respect
26. He treats other men with respect
27. He tells you what he wants, what he likes and what he dislikes and doesn't expect you to read his mind

28. He is patient
29. He makes you feel secure, valued and respected always.
30. He makes you feel that you are the most important thing in his life.
31. You can't envision your future without him

Extra Credit: Add three more of your own "Green Lights"...

32.
33.
34.

That is our "Top 31" Green Light list for how to set your "second husband" (or wife) apart from the other would be suitors in your life. We truly believe that the ideal mate is someone who ticks most of the boxes in our Green Light list, because ultimately you want a relationship in which you feel that you are a better you because he or she is in it and where you feel loved, secure, respected, valued and that you have a true partnership. As with any partnership, to succeed it must be based on trust and a common goal that you both have clearly articulated to one another so your expectations and those of your partner are clear from the beginning. It is also a good idea to check every once in a while to make sure your goals and dreams are still on the same page as you travel through life together.

Remember, according to the U.S. Census Bureau, not only do 52-62% of first marriages end in divorce, but 60% of all remarriages eventually end in divorce as well. We wrote this book to help lower that number and give you simple, easily understood tools to aid you in making the best possible decision as to who to marry, whether it's the first time, the second time or any number at all. After all, the U.S. Census Bureau also revealed that married people have both more and better sex than singles do, that the previously married tend to be considerably less happy and more distressed than the currently married and that married men and women generally live longer than single men and women. If these aren't reasons enough to seek out a compatible life partner, keep in mind that being married should be a primary source of joy, fulfillment and love in your life. It certainly has been for us and that is what we desire for you as well.

CHAPTER THREE

FORTY QUESTIONS FOR A DEEPER DIVE

"A person that never climbs will never fall." — William Shakespeare

Since you already know how much we LOVE lists, we decided that one of the best ways we can help you make the best possible decision when it comes to marrying your "second husband" first, is to provide you with our list of "40 Questions for a Deeper Dive" This gives you a fabulous opportunity to spend some structured time with your partner or potential partner examining how you both feel about some important issues and questions. These are designed to help you uncover how you and your partner feel about life in general, relationships in particular and will hopefully illuminate some of the important ideas, ideals and ways of thinking that you ought to know about each other before making the lifetime commitment of marriage.

Obviously if we were giving you both instructions before tackling these questions, we would simply say be honest in your answers, be open to exploring further any one of the questions as issues present themselves or you discover differences in your outlook on any of them. In addition, do your best to remain nonjudgmental and an active listener which means the willingness to ask for further clarifications as you go to make sure you really do understand what your partner is saying, what he or she is thinking and how he or she is really feeling. One of the greatest challenges in any relationship, especially emotionally charged relationships is the simple challenge of effective communication. It is probably the advice we give to couples more often than any other – when you want to know something about what your partner thinks or how your partner feels, ask questions of each other and then listen, listen, listen until you truly hear the answer. So, without further ado here are our top 40 relationship question suggestions to help you delve deeper with each other. These questions work best when you sit down with each other face to face, read each one out loud and then both respond one at a time and then talk about whatever seems interesting to either of you. What you will need for this exercise: 1) a table, 2) two chairs, 3) a pad and pencil (if you are old) or a smart device (if you are young), 4) two ears each ready to listen….

40 Questions For a Deeper Dive

1. Given the choice of anyone in the world, whom would you want as a dinner guest and why?
2. Would you like to be famous? In what way and why?
3. Would you rather you or your partner die first?
4. What would constitute a "perfect" day for you?
5. When did you last sing to yourself? To someone else?
6. If you were able to live to the age of 90 and retain either the mind or the body of a 30-year-old which would you want and why?
7. Do you have a secret hunch about how you will die?
8. What three things would you most want to have in common with your partner?
9. For what three things in your life do you feel most grateful?
10. If you could change anything about the way you were raised, what would it be?
11. If you could wake up tomorrow having gained any one quality or ability, what would it be?
12. What would you want your super power to be?
13. If a crystal ball could tell you anything about your life, the future or anything else, what would you want to know?
14. Is there something that you've dreamed of doing for a long time? Why haven't you done it?
15. What is the greatest accomplishment of your life?
16. What do you value most in a friendship?
17. What is your most treasured memory?
18. What is your most terrible memory?
19. If you knew that in one year you would die suddenly, what would you change about the way you are now living? Why?
20. What does friendship mean to you?
21. What roles do love and affection play in your life?

22. What are five things you consider a positive characteristic of your partner?
23. How close and warm is your family? Do you feel your childhood was happier than most other people's? Why?
24. How do you feel about your relationship with your mother?
25. Make three true "we" statements each.
26. Complete this sentence: "I love having someone with whom I share ________."
27. What is important for your partner to know about you that he/she doesn't know already?
28. How would you describe your understanding of God?
29. What was an embarrassing moment in your life?
30. When did you last cry in front of another person? By yourself?
31. What are the three most important values you would want to pass on to your children?
32. What, if anything, is too serious to be joked about?
33. If you were to die this evening with no opportunity to communicate with anyone, what would you most regret not having told someone? What is keeping you from telling them?
34. Your house, containing everything you own, catches fire. After saving your loved ones and pets, you have time to safely make a final dash to save any one item. What would it be? Why?

35. Of all the people in your family, whose death would you find most disturbing? Why?
36. Share a personal problem and ask your partner's advice on how he or she might handle it.
37. How important is faith or religion in your life and how involved in your religious tradition are you?
38. Why get married and not just live together?
39. How do you want to be remembered when you die?
40. What are the most important things your partner could do to make you feel safe, secure and loved?
41.
42.
43.

Chapter Four

BETTER TO MARRY YOUR "SECOND HUSBAND" SECOND (OR THIRD, OR EVEN FOURTH) THAN NEVER AT ALL...

"Every heart sings a song incomplete until another heart whispers back."
— Plato

Oh no, not another list! Sigh, we just can't seem to tell you anything without a list can we? We promise, however, that this will be the very last one. After all, we have already given you the "10 Steps to Finding Your Second Husband First" list, the "20 Worst Reasons for Getting Married" list, the "Red Light" and "Green Light" lists, and the "40 Questions to Fall in Love With" list. What list could possibly be left to share? It's the list of lessons to remember what you have already learned from your own personal life experiences with relationships or marriage, even if you made a bad first (or second or third) marriage already. This is the list that will remind you of how far you have come, of how different you are now from when you first began your search for the right partner in the past, how much you have grown as a human being and the special lessons of life you are now bringing to the table as you create this new, better, more fulfilling and successful relationship. Here are the key things to remember:

1. <u>You have now graduated with a degree in "Spouse 101."</u> You are now educated and in a much better place to make a choice of a "Second Husband" than you were when you were looking the first time around. So, okay, maybe you had to go the distance first, but after all, learning and growing is the key to success in any endeavor and any field. No shortcuts for you. No Cliff Notes. You put in the time, paid your dues and now you are ready to embrace the fact that you made the best decision you could at the time, given the information you had.

2. You no longer have to worry about learning from other people's mistakes and bad experiences. You've got your very own to learn from instead! Treasure those lessons and realize that the ones you learn from your own personal experiences are really the best ones, because they are real and belong only to you. You'll see that they actually mean so much more to you than "other people's lesson-to-be-learned" as you start evaluating new relationships in your life. Like, if you are out on a date with someone who does something obnoxious that your "First Husband" did that drove you batty, your inner Red Flag buzzer will go off like a three-alarm fire and you'll be back home nice and comfy on the couch in your PJ's watching TV before you can say, "Hey, would you mind taking me home? I feel a fatal disease coming on and I think it may be contagious."
3. You are not a loser. You mustn't ever let that thought enter your mind. A smart person once said, "As you think, so shall you become." Obviously that person thought he was smart. That's why he was able to come up with such a smart quote. Look, just because you made a bad choice in a "First Husband" doesn't mean you aren't worthy of attracting a winner. It just means you weren't picky enough back "then," but this is "now." Now you know better. Right? Knowing better is a good thing and a reminder that you have grown since then. Thanks to the lessons you learned with your "First Husband," you know what you want and need in a Second Husband. I guess you could say, your first marriage will serve as a kind of "weedwhacker" of possible Second Husbands so don't fret, smile and get ready for the next glorious chapter in your upcoming "Second Husband" marriage.
4. You are not a failure. Hey, remember school? If you got an "F" on a paper or composition or test you could make it up? Besides, even if you did get an "F" once or twice, you still didn't necessarily fail the entire course, right? Well, it's the same thing with marriage. So, you blew the first test. So what. You learn from it and get to try again on the next test. You get to do a "make-up" test so to speak. A "do over." Everybody gets an "F" in something, one time or another. Some folks more than once and more than others. But hey, every failure in life is another step toward success. Just remember, YOU are not a failure. You may fail now and again, but that does not make YOU a failure, ever. See the difference? Good.
5. You are one step ahead of those who still have to figure out how to marry their "Second Husband" first. After all, you've already "been there and done that" so you can go straight to your "Second Husband" a heck of a lot easier from here. Chances of your marrying yet another "First Husband" are much slimmer, although not out of the question, so don't get to thinking you're "all that" girlfriend, 'cause you are still human and quite capable of forgetting all those valuable lessons

you managed not to absorb in "Marriage #1." There is absolutely no room for complacency in matters of the heart – ever! So, pay attention in First Marriage School. You really don't want to have to take that class all over again now, do you?

6. You're older and wiser and more in touch with what you want in a life partner. The "olderer" and "wiserer" you get the more likely you are to marry a pretty darned good "Second Husband." You are also a helluva lot choosier as well. When you are younger you figure, "Hey, I'm young and stupid, I can marry someone who is just OK and it will all work out. I'll just fix whatever's wrong with him anyway. So, what if he is a baseball fanatic and I think of baseball as a game for people who are completely brain dead. And it's sooo boring. I can put up with brain death can't I?" When you are older and wiser you say, "Hey, I'm older and wiser now and while brain death was possible to live with, it wasn't that much fun either, so now I think I want to have fun with a mate who can actually string two words together and communicate other than with grunts holding a remote control in one hand and a beer in the other."

7. You are not as much in a hurry to marry this time as you were the first time. Back to that biological clock thing. If you have already had kids, then it's not ticking anymore (hopefully) so you can relax now and take your time as you learn more and more about Mr. Potential Second Husband. Unfortunately, so many first marriages grow out of that urgent need and desire for children and not primarily because a couple love each other. The best reason to marry someone is that you believe in your heart of hearts that you simply cannot imagine life without that person at your side. It is an undeniable reality that the desire for children seriously clouds one's vision as it pertains to the search for a true soul mate. That's why second marriages in our opinion can still have a better chance of lasting a lifetime. With that urgency surrounding the need to have children no longer the driving force in your search for a partner, you can devote yourself to finding the partner that you should have married in the first place. Use the two-year rule. Go together for a year before you get engaged and then another year till you marry. What's the rush? You've had your kids, remember so that ship has sailed.
8. You are more careful and thoughtful in your choices of possible "Second Husbands." That's because you are a helluva lot smarter now than you were then. It's amazing how the mistakes of a First Marriage seem to become the very tools with which you can build a successful Second Marriage. Of course, there are those certain divorced individuals who you might hear say, "Well. That was a waste of time!" as they speak about their First Marriage. Sorry, but those people are just stupid. Verrrry stupid. Muy estupido. It's actually downright scary how stupid that is. Why? Because "as you think so shall you become." If you think and believe that it was a waste, then, indeed, it was and is a waste. What a waste to think of such treasures as the lessons of a failed First Marriage… as a waste! That would be like throwing the prize away with the Crackerjacks and just keeping the empty box. Now, hey, is that a smart thing, ever?
9. You, yourself are more evolved as a human being now than you were then. The list of qualities you are looking for in a "Second Husband" no doubt looks quite different now than it did back when you were, shall we say, a less evolved human being in your twenties. Back "then" your "Things I Absolutely Can't Live Without in a Life Partner" list probably included qualities like, great body, blue eyes, brown eyes, eyes, curly hair, long hair, hairless, a large, really large, fat, big, huge bank account (what you were thinking something else?), cooks, can make love for at least six hours straight without ever having to stop for a sandwich, can score great drugs….Today, your more evolved-as-a-human list might include such qualities as easy enough on the eyes, can walk without a cane, loves to spend hours by the fire, the oceanfront, under the stars as long as

those hours are with me, loves to muse at museums, concerts, art exhibits, science fairs, loves to travel, go to shows, loves animals, is philanthropic, is generous and fun loving and has a large, really, really large, fat, big, huge bank account (OK, some things don't evolve as fast).

10. Keep in mind at all times the definition of insanity. Insanity is doing the same thing over and over and over again and expecting a different result.

Chapter Five

CONCLUSION... WHERE YOU GO FROM HERE

"Goodness is the only investment that never fails."
— Henry David Thoreau

Well that's it. We come to the end of our book and believe it or not, the end of our lists. When all is said and done, not only this last list, but the entire book has been our desire to remind you that you are competent, worthy and deserving of love. You deserve to be happy. You deserve to be treated with respect. You deserve to be loved and valued. Tell yourself that every single day when you look in the mirror and definitely before you go on any date and even more definitely before you accept any marriage proposal. This book has been our way of reminding you of your fundamental spiritual self-worth, and what our particular religious tradition (Judaism) has always taught us in the very beginning of the Bible by saying that every human being is created in the divine image. It means you count. What you say matters. What you do matters. Who you are matters. You are worthy and deserving of having a joyful, fulfilling, love-filled life. Yes, that is really why we wrote this short book – to remind you of your own self-worth and hopefully help you create the loving, successful relationship you have always deserved. We'd love to hear about your journey and your successes, (and share your "extra credit" lists as well) so feel free to let us know what your own search has produced in your life.

Where do you go from here? You put yourself out there into the world of creating relationships, of opening up to self-discovery, of exploring endless possibilities of adding meaning and purpose to your life through creating loving, nurturing, inspiring relationships whether they end up in marriage of simply expanding your personal community of friends and life supporters. The wise ancient Chinese philosopher Lao Tzu, who lived and taught over 2,500 years ago wrote in the famous Tao Te Ching, "New beginnings are often disguised as painful endings." It isn't always easy to strike out on a new path in life, to put yourself out in the world knowing that you are opening up your heart to the possibility of heartache as well as the opportunity for joy and fulfillment. Still it is always true that only by taking the risk that you might experience pain or disappointment can you be in a position to find the thrill and excitement of discovering a relationship that can make your dreams come true. We are excited to be a part of your journey and hope you will share with us not only the trials and tribulations, but the triumphs and successes of this precious journey as well. We leave you with the beautiful words of the poet Emily Dickinson which have inspired us to write this book and share our passion for creating successful, loving relationships with you:

"If I can stop one heart from breaking, I shall not live in vain."
— Emily Dickinson

Didi Carr Reuben is proud to have been the rebbetzin of Kehillat Israel Reconstructionist Congregation in Pacific Palisades, California for the past 34 years. She is a singer and actress who has performed around the world and starred in her own sitcom, Sugartime on ABC-TV, and for many years wrote a regular relationships advice column entitled, "Ask the Rebbetzin."

Steven Carr Reuben is senior rabbi emeritus of Kehillat Israel Reconstructionist Congregation in Pacific Palisades, California, past president of the Board of Rabbis of Southern California, the recipient of numerous community awards, including the Micah Award for founding the largest full-service homeless shelter in Los Angeles, and the Unsung Heroes Award from the Youth Law Center of San Francisco, and is the author of numerous books, including Children of Character: Leading Your Children to Ethical Choices in Everyday Life and A Nonjudgmental Guide to Interfaith Marriage.

Seth Mallios (illustrator) is Professor of Anthropology, University History Curator, and Director of the South Coastal Information Center at San Diego State University where he has spearheaded six active research projects resulting in nine books including Born a Slave, Died a Pioneer. His illustrations appear weekly in the on-line word puzzle, Re:Punzle.

Notes

Notes

Printed in the United States
By Bookmasters